Ibiza
● Formentera

EVEREST

Text: Carlos J. Taranilla de la Varga

Photographs: Ángel Segura
Georama (p. 8-9, 15, 16b, 24-25, 27, 28b, 40-41, 55)
Joan A. Parés (p. 22, 23, 39, 47b, 53, 54, 65)
Triangle (p. 42-43, 56-57)

Design and Layout: Gerardo Rodera

Cover design: Alfredo Anievas

Translated by EURO:TEXT (Martin Gell)

© EDITORIAL EVEREST, S.A.
Carretera León-La Coruña, km 5 - LEÓN
ISBN-Number: 84-241-3668-3
Legal deposit: LE. 289-1996
Printed in Spain

EDITORIAL EVERGRÁFICAS, S.L.
Carretera León-La Coruña, km 5
LEON (Spain)

THE ISLAND OF IBIZA

The island of Ibiza has a surface area of 521.22 km^2 and a population of around 50,000. The third largest of the islands comprising the Balearic archipelago in the Mediterranean sea, it features a maximum length of 41 km. Its highest point is at Sa Talaiassa, which stands at 475 m. Other elevations worthy of note are Puig Furnás (409 m), Puig Camp Vey (399 m), Puig d'en Capitá (385 m), Atalaya (361 m) and Puig Nonó (258 m).

In the northwest, Ibiza's coastline is one of sheer cliffs, whereas in the remaining areas it is characterized by a succession of coves, bays and extensive stretches of sand such as that of the *D'en Bossa* beach in the southeast. Situated in the south of the island is a coastal plain featuring the famous salt mines that have been operating since ancient times. Lying to the south, east and west of Ibiza are many islands, such as Es Vedrá, Es Penjats, Espalmador, Espardell, Tagomago and Conillera.

One of the famous beaches of Ibiza.

*Above, orange trees at Sant Miquel. On the facing page, almond trees in bloom
and a country woman or 'payesa' at work.*

As far as plant-life on Ibiza is concerned, there is an abundance of pines, savines, carobs, olives, almonds and fig trees, as well as numerous slender palm trees. In spring, the countryside is to be seen in all its glory and blossom appears everywhere, above all on almond-tree branches, which afford a true spectacle of colour.

Ibiza's climate is a very pleasant one, temperatures varying very little and rainfall being scarce. The island is protected by its mountainous relief, which provides shelter from the winds. Even in winter it is graced with long spells of fair weather and many are the days on which one can go for a swim in the sea. The sun, the blue sea and the calm horizon are almost permanent features of the Ibizan scenery.

Rural dwelling on Ibiza.

The scenery of Ibiza is dotted with typical rural dwellings whose geometrical forms stand in harmony with nature. Small in size, they feature flat roofs —due to the lack of rain— and have few openings, in order to keep the heat out. At the entrance, they normally have a *porxo*, a place where one can sit and rest awhile. Being whitewashed from top to bottom, these dwellings lend a characteristic touch to the island's scenery. Santiago Rusignol once called Ibiza *la isla blanca*, the white island, the name it is given in tourist circles and which constitutes one of its most beautiful, world-renowned advertisements. Indeed, the inspiration for many present-day buildings has been found in the traditional rural dwelling.

Necropolis on Puig des Molins.

THE HISTORY OF IBIZA

The island of Ibiza was first inhabited as far back as prehistoric times. Subsequently, it was colonized by the Greeks, who gave this island and neighbouring Formentera the name of *Islas Pitiusas* in allusion to the abundance of pines to be found here. The Carthaginians called the island *Ibossim*, and the Romans *Ebusus*. At a later date, upon the conquest of the island by the Moors, it came to be known as *Yebisah*, which is the origin of its present-day name. Clearly bearing witness to the Punic presence on Ibiza are a large number of terracotta figurines representing Carthaginian deities —the goddess Tanit, the god Bes—, as well as charms, sacred necklaces, funerary masks, zoomorphic ceramic articles, jewels, stamps, sacred vases made of polychrome ostrich eggs and a series of coins minted on Ibiza featuring the head of the god Bes on one of their sides. Most of these objects were found at the necropolis on the Puig des Molins or were unearthed at the excavations carried out at Illa Plana and in the Es Cuieram cave.

*Above, 'hippies' at the
Es Canar street market.
Right, fishing from a jetty.*

*Preceding two-page spread,
a view of the city of Ibiza and its
'Dalt Vila' or old quarter.*

Rome granted the islands of Ibiza and
Formentera the status of *Confederate City*,
whereby they were able to maintain certain
privileges —they retained their own jurisdiction
and religious beliefs and were exempt from
sending men to serve in the Roman legions, even
though they had to provide auxiliary troops. The
Romans, in keeping with their interest in public
works, brought drinkable water to the capital
town and built several aqueducts. As late as the
18th century we find references to one or other
of these structures on the road from Ibiza to Ses
Salines, at Santa Eulària and Santa Gertrudis.
The Moslems, who so carefully went about their
agricultural activities, created a network of
irrigation ditches at 'Ses Feixes', near to the
present-day Ibiza-Sant Joan road. In the field of
the arts, the period of Moslem rule saw the rise
to fame of the Ibizan poet Idris Ibn Al-Yamani,
referred to as 'Al Sabini' in allusion to the savines
that dominate the island scenery.
On 8th August 1235, Ibiza was reconquered by
Catalan troops during the reign of King James I
(the 'Conqueror'), who, in the form of a feudal
donation, entrusted this military undertaking to
Guillermo de Montgrí, the archbishop of
Tarragona, who was joined on the expedition by
Prince Pedro of Portugal and Nuño Sans, count
of El Rosellón.

*Defence
tower.*

Once the island had been reconquered, it was divided into five areas called *quartones*, namely Ses Salines, Santa Eulària, Portmany, Balanzat and Llano de la Villa. The conquerors granted the islanders a series of rights and privileges, such as exemption from taxes, free trade, dispensation from providing military services and the inviolability of the home.

Up to the 19th century, Ibiza and Formentera constituted a single municipality, known under the name of *Universidad*, which comprised a Secret Council and a General Council. On the former sat the representatives of the three social strata or *Manos*: the *Mano Mayor* (gentlemen), the *Mano Menor* (sailors and craftsmen) and the *Mano Foránea* (the peasants). The purpose of this council was to deal with the ordinary, everyday matters and issues that arose concerning life on the island. The General Council was primarily responsible for the drawing up of the annual accounts, apart from which it also managed issues of certain political importance. Councillors were elected by the so-called *saco y suerte* system, whereby for each of the above-mentioned *manos* or social strata a series of names were drawn out of a sack at random.

The island Governor acted as judge and was assisted in this role by a lawyer. Remedies of appeal were granted before a commissioned judge and, in the last resort, before the Viceroy of Majorca. No direct intervention in island affairs was made by the monarchy until the construction of the capital's new walls, which were begun by Charles V in 1554 and completed by Philip II in 1585.

A vital element of Ibiza's defences were its watch-towers. Scattered all around the island, they played a decisive role in the fight against piracy, an all-too-common threat to these shores.

Since the mid-19th century, Ibiza has been divided into five municipalities: the capital, Ibiza; Sant Antoni; Sant Josep; Sant Joan de Labritja; and Santa Eulària d'es Riu. The fact that each of these towns bears the name of a saint - which tourists inevitably find surprising - is due to their having taken on the name of the parish around which their first houses originally sprang up.

Nowadays Ibiza and Formentera come under the same judicial district and since the system of self-governing regions was established in Spain belong to the Autonomous Community of the Balearic Islands.

Two sporting options on the island of Ibiza: hang-gliding and golf.

Typical Ibizan musical instruments.

Basketwork shop. ▶

FOLKLORE AND HANDICRAFTS

Ibiza is an island steeped in folklore. The most characteristic of the traditional local costumes for women is the *gonella*, which consists of a ground-length pleated black woollen tunic; a pinafore, likewise made of wool, embroidered and featuring a bodice with detachable sleeves; a shawl placed over the shoulders and brought together at the chest; and a headscarf. When in costume the women wear pita-fibre espadrilles with esparto soles and high, closed ends. On their arms they carry the *abrigai*, a small deep-red cape. To complete their attire they adorn themselves with a large number of jewels and matching accessories. Also noteworthy is the *traje blanco* or white dress, which differs from the *gonella* in that the black woollen tunic is replaced by a white puffed up skirt with several underlayers. The typical island costume for men comprises white linen trousers (in summer) or black worsted ones (in winter), tight at the feet and around the legs but loose and pleated at the waist, where a red or black sash is worn. The men wear white shirts with stand-up collars and black waistcoats featuring two rows of buttons on either side. They too wear pita-fibre espadrilles, but unlike those worn by the women, theirs have open ends. On their heads they sport red hats with black turn-ups that are reminiscent of crests, as a result of which this typical costume is known as *el gallo* (the cock), the name which by extension is also given to the person wearing it.

*Ceramist at
Sant Rafael.*

Espardenyes.

*Weaving
espardenyes.*

The typical Ibizan dance is one of two times, the *curta* and the *llarga* (the short and the long). In the first, short time the woman traces little figure eights whilst the man, facing her at every moment, follows her by means of little leaps. In the long time, the woman traces wider circles and the man, taking great bounds (thus living up to the nickname we mentioned before: 'the cockerel') and playing the castanets, seeks out the face of his partner, who at times seems to shy away from him. At the end of the dance, the man passes his arms over his partner's head and bends his knees before her in a gesture of surrender. The dance is accompanied by a variety of typical musical instruments, such as the oleander flute; a well-adorned drum; large juniper castanets; and a little steel sword that marks out the time. Besides these typical island dances, one must not overlook the deep-rooted rural customs such as the *festeig*, the occasion on which all the fathers with daughters at a marriagable age would have the local lads come visit their houses; the latter would go from one house to the next in search of a wife. In the presence of her father, each young lady would enter a room where all the young men were waiting and would sit on a chair next to which another was placed so that the hopeful lads could one by one sit and talk to the girl and make plans for their future marriage. When in this way one of the couples came to an agreement, the fiancée would appear at mass on the following Sunday wearing rings on all her fingers —but not on her thumbs— and carrying a key and a heart linked by a chain.

Typical hats.

Typical costume. ▶

Apart from the above-mentioned musical instruments, other noteworthy Ibizan handicrafts are the local ceramics and glass; hand-embroidered articles; woollen jumpers and the traditional objects made of palm, straw, esparto and pita such as hats, baskets and espadrilles or *espardenyes*. Another highlight is the luxurious world of island jewellery, although faced by the enormous variety of items on offer, one must understandably make sure they are genuine. Meriting special attention is the typical Ibizan 'ad lib' fashion (*ad libitum*: dress as you wish), which perhaps more than anything else indicates the special sense of independence that is to be felt on the island. A large number of shops cater for this fashion, which is also to be seen alongside the abundance of handicrafts at the street markets of Sant Antoni (Fridays), Sant Miquel (Thursdays), and Santa Eulària (at Punta Arabí, Wednesdays) and at the boutiques awaiting one at every turn. Neither should one forget the market stands run by hippies, who settled on the island as from the nineteen-sixties and today remain true to their particular way of life (a kind of genuine philosophy), making a series of unusual objects which they sell to the tourists.

Typical examples of Balearic cuisine.

GASTRONOMY

As one would expect, not forgetting that we are on a beautiful little Mediterranean island, Ibizan cuisine is deeply rooted in its own environment and is dominated by products from the rural world and the sea. As is the case practically throughout the 'Mare Nostrum', Ibiza boasts a great variety of generally high-quality fish and seafood. *Guisat de peix* is a dish made with fish accompanied by garlic, onion, tomato, saffron, parsley, potatoes, cinnamon, olive oil and salt. The most characteristic seafood dishes are the *burrida de rajada* (ray), cuttlefish *a la marinera*, Ibiza-style lobster, octopus with peppers and *tonyina a l'eivissenca*, tuna seasoned with raisins, eggs, pine kernels, spices, white wine and lemon.

As far as meats are concerned, the following are to be recommended: *llom de porc* or loin of pork; *costelletes de moltó* or lamb ribs, roasted with mushrooms; *conill amb pebrots vermells* (rabbit with red peppers); as well as *perdíus amb col* (partridges with cabbage), and the *sofrit pagès* or the sautéed *sobrassada i botifarrons* (spicy pork sausagemeat) with pork fat, potatoes and chicken broth.

Amongst the stews and casseroles to be savoured are the *olla fresca* (broad and haricot beans, potatoes and a couple of pears) or the *caragols* (snails cooked with cold meats and pork fat); and the *cuinat de Quaresma* or haricot bean and vetch stew. Other tasty dishes are *truita pagesa* (potato omelette with peppers and tomatoes), *sopa de menuts* (chicken giblet soup), and *arrós sec* (rice with rabbit, chicken, mussels and prawns).

If one should wish to try a local wine, then there is the red or white *vi de taula pagès*. The highlights of island confectionery, apart from the traditional Balearic *sobrassadas*, are the *flaons* (made from flour, eggs, cheese, sugar and aniseed) and the so-called *macarrons de Sant Joan*. On Formentera one simply has to try the *pensats i fets*, exquisite traditional pastries.

Two views of the old quarter of Ibiza. Two-page spread overleaf, Ibiza from the sea.

THE TOWN OF IBIZA (EIVISSA)

Ibiza was founded by the Carthaginians in 654 B.C. on a fortified hill protected by the sea, in the image of other cities of Punic foundation such as Cagliari in Italy or Carthage itself. Following on from the accounts of Timeo (4th-3rd century B.C.), Diodoro Siculo (1st century B.C.) reports that the town had 'extensive walls and splendid houses, with inhabitants from different races although predominantly Carthaginian'. Consequently, the Punic influence was to be felt in Ibiza right up to the times of the Roman Empire.

The Carthaginian *Ibossim*, the Roman *Ebusus*, the Moslem *Yebisah* and the Ibiza or Eivissa we know today has always been a town divided into two very different parts, namely the high-lying quarter called *Dalt Vila* (the old town), standing at the heart of the walled enclosure like an acropolis or fortified city, and the modern district that, starting from the seafront, stretches out at a lower level. In addition to this we have the Sa Penya district which, as its name would suggest, rises up over a craggy cliff between the quay and the old bastion of Santa Lucía, providing inspiration for artists and poets. Sa Penya comprises an intricate network of narrow streets (like *Sa Drassaneta*) and huddled dwellings inhabited by seafaring people and fishermen that lend a characteristic flavour to the area.

*Different views
of Dalt Vila.*

To be found in the Dalt Vila area are the buildings of greatest artistic interest in Ibiza, the most outstanding example of which is the *Santa María de las Nieves* Cathedral which, built in Gothic style in the 13th and 14th centuries on the site formerly occupied by a mosque, underwent reconstruction in the 18th century. Elements still remaining from its original structure are the bell tower and the sacristy doorway, whilst the most significant of its artistic treasures are a 15th-century monstrance featuring a relic of the True Cross, some (15th-century) Gothic panels depicting St James and St Matthew, and a Renaissance relief of the Virgin of the Rosary. Flanking the cathedral square are the ancient curia with its Gothic doorway, the Archaeological Museum — containing one of the most important collections of Punic art— and the castle, mentioned by Tito Livio as early as the 3rd century and again by Ruiz González de Clavijo in 1403. The Santo Domingo monastery, whose construction was begun in the 16th century, today houses the Town Hall; an outstanding feature of the old monastery church is the baroque altarpiece in the Rosary chapel.

Two views of the Santa María Cathedral in Ibiza.

Monument to Vara de Rey.

Portal de las Tablas.

The following buildings are well worth a visit in Ibiza: the *San Cristóbal* church and monastery (17th-century); the old *Iglesia del Patrocinio*, a church dating from the 15th century and also referred to as *Iglesia del Hospitalet*; the 13th-century episcopal palace; and some of the residences that once belonged to the nobility. Of equal interest is the Museum of Contemporary Art, likewise in Dalt Vila, which displays modern painting and sculpture, and neither should one overlook the various exhibition halls and the countless shops dealing in handicrafts and antiques. The walled enclosure, the work of the engineer Juan Bautista Calvi and Jacopo Palcaro (called Frantin), was begun in 1554 during the reign of Emperor Charles V and completed in 1585 under Philip II. In 1942, the walls were declared a Monument of National Interest. They feature seven bastions (those named Santa Tecla, San Bernardo, San Jorge, Santiago, San Juan, Santa Lucía and Puerta Nueva or Portal Nou) and three entrance gateways, the most important of which is the *Portal de las Tablas*, flanked by two Roman statues. This gate is crowned by the Habsburg coat of arms and an inscription recording the date on which work on the walls was completed, 1585, and the reigning monarch of the day, Philip II . Passing through the gateway, one comes into the former Parade Ground. The other two gateways to the walled enclosure are the Portal Nou and the Puerta de Sant Joan. The 19th century witnessed the beginnings of what would be the modern extension of the town, which spread out towards the roads to Sant Antoni and Sant Josep. The main axis along which this occurred was the Paseo de Vara de Rey, an avenue at the centre of which lies the monument to the memory of General Vara de Rey, the Ibizan military hero who achieved glory in the Cuban War of 1898. The monument was unveiled by King Alfonso XIII on 4th April 1904. In 1906 the Obelisk to the Privateers or *Corsarios* was erected, in commemoration of the Ibizan captain Antonio Riquer Arabí, who a century earlier in 1806 had achieved great renown amongst the island privateers due to his having captured the English brigantine *Felicity*.

In line with the great tourist boom of the last few decades and the subsequent increase in population, the town of Ibiza has spread out beyond its former limits, a series of new districts having sprung up, such as Ses Figueretes, which has arisen around the beach of the same name, a beach now lined with hotels, apartments and other establishments catering for tourists.

To be found in the low-lying modern part of the town that stretches out from the seafront is the shopping district featuring an abundance of different kinds of shops, together with numerous souvenir shops offering the tourist a wide range of mementoes. The seafront, *La Marina*, is a clean, well-kept, beautiful area whose buildings are of the classical Ibizan style with their ever-present whitewashed façades. Not far from the town lies the Puig des Molins Carthaginian necropolis, the archaeological excavations of which first began in

Monument to the Privateers.

Street in the old quarter.

1903. Apart from the numerous figurines crafted in terracotta (baked, glazed and polychrome clay) and dedicated to the goddess Tanit, and a series of ritual objects, funerary masks, sacred vases, charms and the like, all of which can be seen at the necropolis' very own Monographical Museum, the most significant finds to be made here were the hypogea or burial chambers containing dishes laid out for the survival of the dead beyond the grave, a clear testimony of the beliefs held by the Carthaginians.

Another surprise for the people of Ibiza was the gradual arrival on the island of the hippie movement in the nineteen sixties. Nowadays, however, the hippies have become part and parcel of the island scene. They are forever present in the town, especially in the port area and the old quarter. One of their favourite haunts is the *Portal de la Tablas*, and this is where they offer the tourists their 'typical' products. Ibiza, both the town and the island as a whole, has always offered a warm welcome to all those who have found their way here —to the colonizers and *conquistadores* of the past and the international tourists of the present.

Ibiza town is simply brimming with bars, discotheques and night clubs, and even boasts a casino with international gambling rooms, located on the promenade. It also has a racecourse, a flying club (*Real Aeroclub*), a 300-berth sailing club (*Club Náutico*) and the 539-berth marina (*Puerto Deportivo Nueva Ibiza*). There is a waterpark, Aquamar, at D'en Bossa beach, and many other tourist attractions. Craft shops and art galleries abound along the streets of Ibiza. From the 4th to the 8th August, the town celebrates the festivities of its patron saint, Our Lady of the Snows (a seemingly strange choice, since it very rarely snows on Ibiza), in commemoration of the Christian reconquest of the island.

Talamanca beach.

Figueretas beach.

Street in Sant Antoni de Portmany.

SANT ANTONI DE PORTMANY
(SAN ANTONIO ABAD)

Sant Antoni, situated 16 km from the capital Ibiza, is together with Santa Eulària d'es Riu the second most important town on the island and has a population of around 15,000. The Romans gave the name of Portus Magnus to the town's beautiful bay, a natural inlet. The Moors called it Portumany, a toponym which subsequently in the Middle Ages evolved into 'Portmany'. In 1383 the settlement here was sacked and razed to the ground by Turkish pirates.

Today, Sant Antoni is a cosmopolitan town bristling with hotels, bungalows and tourist developments, along with restaurants, bars, discotheques and other entertainment spots. Its port has sea-route connections with Formentera, Ibiza and Denia (Alicante) and boasts a 204-berth sailing club-marina. Rising up on the promenade is a monument to the town's fishermen; the local peasants are likewise commemorated by a monument on the corner of *Calle Ramón y Cajal* and *Carrer Ample.* The festivities held in celebration of St Antony, the town's patron saint, take place on 17th January and every Friday there is a typical market at Sa Tanca.

Built in the 14th century, Sant Antoni's parish church was endowed with defensive elements in order to afford resistance to raids by pirates.

The port at Sant Antoni.

Santa Agnes basilica.

*Port des Torrent.
Beach.*

*Cala
Salada.*

*Detail of the
Church of Sant
Rafael.* ▶

Lying 2 km from Sant Antoni is the Palaeochristian basilica of Santa Agnes, which has been restored and declared a Monument of National Interest.

About 5 km to the north, in the vicinity of Cap Nonó, we come across the cave of Ses Fontanelles, which contains interesting Bronze age paintings.

However, the real attraction of Sant Antoni and its surrounding area are the coves and beaches to be found nearby. Cala Bassa, Cala Gració, Cala Salada, Port des Torrent and even Portinatx —all are very cosmopolitan and of great natural beauty, have fine sand and crystal-clear waters and are best reached not by car but by boat. The sunsets to be enjoyed in Portmany bay are truly majestic, with the Isla Sa Conillera (Warren Island) in the background. As legend will have it, it was on this island that the Carthaginian general Hannibal was born. Also lying close-by are the beaches of Es Puet, Ses Savines and Pinet.

SANTA EULÀRIA D'ES RIU

Situated 15 km from the capital on the eastern side of the island, Santa Eulària lies at the foot of the Puig de Missa, on the banks of the river that bears its name. *Río Santa Eulària* is the only true river in all the Balearics, even though it is only 11 km long. The town's parish church was built in 1568 and, like all the others to be seen on the island, affords a distinctly defensive appearance. It was erected over a 14th-century chapel that had been demolished by Turkish pirates. Featuring a noteworthy apsidal tower, the church has been declared an Item of Cultural Interest. The new town, which has around 16 or 17 thousand inhabitants, comprises a succession of tourist developments at the foot of the Puig de Missa and has spread out along the coast, flanking the promenade. Santa Eulària's port has a 740-berth sailing club, the *Club Náutico*. From here there are sea-route connections to Ibiza and Sant Antoni, as well as to Es Canar and Punta Arabí (scene of the characteristic island markets frequented by the omnipresent hippie population). The festivities in honour of the town's patron saint, St Eulalie, take place on 12th February and include a variety of cultural and sporting activities. Nevertheless, what truly appeals to tourists in this area is the scenery, the coves and the excellent beaches of fine sand. Nestling between Punta Arabí and Cap Roig is Es Canar beach which, like the those at Cala Llonga, Siesta, S'Argamassa and Roca Llisa, affords calm, clear waters. The best testimony to the unrivalled beauty of this area is the continuous stream of tourists that flock here. If we now make our way back to Ibiza capital, shortly before we arrive (about 2 km away) we come across the *Iglesia de Nuestra Señora de Jesús*, a church that contains an important pictorial altarpiece dating from the late 15th or the early 16th century, the work of Rodrigo de Osuna, a painter belonging to the Valencia school.

On the preceding page, Santa Eulària promenade.
Above these lines, Puig de Missa.

Two-page spread overleaf, Ses Salines.

*Above these lines, Es Canar port
and Cala Jondal.*

Right, Sa Caleta.

Cala Boitx.   Cala Llonga.   *Detail of the Church of Sant Josep.* ▶

Above these lines, Church of Sant Jordi. On the facing page, Cala Vedella and the Church of Sant Francesc at Ses Salines (dedicated to St Francis of Paola).

SANT JOSEP (SAN JOSÉ)

The town of Sant Josep lies inland, some 15 km from Ibiza, and has a population of around 10,000. The Sant Josep parish church dates back to the 16th century and its high altapiece was restored after the 1936 Spanish Civil War. The Church of Sant Francesc (St Francis of Paola) at Ses Salines and the Church of Sant Jordi on the road from Ibiza to Ses Salines, constitute fine examples —particularly the latter— of battlemented fortified churches. The festivities held in honour of the town's patron saint, St Joseph, are on 19th March.

The beaches and coves most frequented by tourists are, amongst others, Cala Tarida, Cala Conta, Cala Vedella and Cala d'Hort. Fishing is a very popular sport here, both in its traditional and underwater varieties. Looking out from Sa Talaiassa, which at 475 m is the highest point on the island, one can admire the breathtaking island of Es Vedrá, standing out against the blue sea.

Cala Conta, along with the Illa des Bosc.　　　　*Below, the island of Es Vedrá, looms up in the distance.*

Cala Molí.

Cala Mastella.

Heap of salt.

Discotheque.

Sa Conillera.

Cala d'Hort.

Pou des Lleó.

Cala Llenya.

View of Sant Llorenç. ▶

SES SALINES AND THE AIRPORT

The renowned Ses Salines salt marshes were first worked by the Carthaginians and, subsequent to the reconquest of Ibiza, were donated by King James I to the archbishop of Tarragona, Guillermo de Montgrí. The latter in turn entrusted the islanders with the exploitation of the marshes. Salt in those days was of course a very highly valued commodity (it should not be forgotten that in former times payments were often made in salt, hence the term 'salary'). Indeed, to quote the words of the historian Braudel, Ibiza is the 'island of salt'. The marshes have a yearly output of 80,000 mt, most of which is exported to Nordic countries such as Iceland and Norway. Such production is made possible, amongst other reasons, by the impermeable nature of the soil and the intense sunshine, which entails a high rate of evaporation, namely 1,200 l/m^2. Occupying as they do an area of around 400 ha, in 1871 the salt marshes were sold by the State to a private enterprise for 1,162,000 pesetas.
Lying near the port of Ibiza is the international airport of Es Codolar, the main destination for tourists arriving on the island.

SANT JOAN DE LABRITJA (SAN JUAN BAUTISTA)

The municipality of Sant Joan, situated at about 22 km from Ibiza in the north of the island, encompasses four parishes, namely Sant Joan, Sant Miquel, Sant Llorenç and Sant Vicente Ferrer. The town boasts an 18th-century porticoed church which, initially built as from 1730, has subsequently undergone alterations. Its bell tower dates from the year 1900. On 24th June the celebrations marking the feast day of St John, the town's patron saint, take place. Enormous bonfires are lit the night before and on the day itself there are a series of folk events (such as the typical dances called *ballades*).

◀ *Church of Sant Miquel de Balansat.*

   Two-page spread overleaf, a view of Portinatx.

Church of Sant Llorenç.   Sant Vicenç de Sa Cala. ▶

Cala Sant Vicenç.

At Sant Llorenç one can visit the fortified settlement called Balàfia, a group of rural houses featuring battlemented towers built in order to provide protection against the pirate raids of times gone by.
The festivities held in honour of the local patron saint take place on 12th August and feature a variety of folk events such as the *ball pagès* dance. In the vicinity of Cala San Vicente (or Sant Vicenç), at Es Cuieram, a Carthaginian sanctuary was discovered in 1907. It contained an abundance of objects used in worship, votive offerings and terracotta figurines, all of which can be seen at the Puig des Molins Museum, along with many other vestiges of the Punic culture.
From Sant Vicenç (Sa Cala), there is a nice sea trip to the island of Tagomago, whose sole inhabitants are its falcons, cormorants and seagulls. The island has an altitude of over 100 m.
This is perhaps the most impressive area on Ibiza, due to its many rugged natural spots of incomparable wildness, such as Na Xamena, Port de San Miguel and Cala Portinatx. Elsewhere, the land is seen to slope down to the sea, giving rise to coves of enormous beauty, such as Cala Xarraca.

Above, Sant Miquel; below, Portinatx beach.

Boats that sail from Ibiza to Formentera.

FORMENTERA

Formentera has a surface area of 82.8 km² and a population of around 5,000. Lying about 6 km to the south of Ibiza, it is separated from the latter by the Es Freus strait, itself studded by a series of small islands: Es Penjats (Isla Ahorcados), Espardell, Espalmador, Espardelló. The island's maximum east to west extension is no more than 14 km. Notable topographical elevations are to be found in the south of Formentera, such as La Mola, which at 202 m is the highest point on the island. Rising up to the west at Cap de Barbaria (Cape of Berbería) is Puig Guillem, which stands at 107 m. In the northern half of the island, we come across two lagoons, *Estany des Peix* and *Estany Pudent*, the latter being adjacent to some previously highly productive salt marshes that today have been all but abandoned. Situated between the two lagoons is the island's only port, La Savina. Formentera's climate is a mild and pleasant one, similar to that of Ibiza and characterized by scarce rainfall and temperatures that barely fluctuate. Its landscape is dominated by dry-farming crops (cereals and olives) and also features certain fruit trees such as carobs, figs and almonds, along with the occasional pine or savine wood.

Bicycles for hire at La Savina.

*La Mola cliffs
and lighthouse.*

The belief that Formentera was inhabited as far back as the Bronze Age is founded on the discovery of some remains in 1907 and the recent appearance of a dolmen, the only one on *Las Pitiusas*, similar in characteristics to those of the larger Balearic islands. In ancient times, Formentera was known under the name of *Ofiusa* ('the island of snakes'). Having been called *Pitiusa* - a term encompassing neighbouring Ibiza - by the Greeks, the Romans referred to the island as *Frumentaria* ('island rich in wheat'), whence the present-day name has evolved. In 1246, subsequent to the Christian reconquest, Guillem de Motgrí handed over possession of Formentera to Berenguer Renart. Later on in its history, the island was uninhabited for a certain period, but by the late 18th century had attained a population of over 1,000. The modern stage of its development, one marked by change, began this century with the exploitation of the fishing industry and the salt marshes. Recently, the modernization process undergone by Formentera has reached new heights as a result of the boom in tourism. There are four towns on the island: Sant Francesc Xavier (San Francisco Javier), its capital and the sole administrative district, San Fernando, El Pilar and La Savina, the port at which boats arrive from Ibiza, Sant Antoni and Santa Eulària (only in summer).

Plaque in memory of Jules Verne at La Mola.

Estany del Peix.

Traditional country dances at Sant Francesc Xavier.

The journey to La Savina, which according to the type of boat can last between half an hour to an hour, is a marvellous one, taking one as it does through a cluster of islands. Although a series of bus lines cater for inland transport on Formentera, many tourists prefer to hire bicycles and calmly ride around this most laid-back of islands. There are two sailing clubs here: the Marina de Formentera, boasting 114 berths, and the 30-berth Puerto de Formentera. Needless to say, the visitor to the island can indulge in water sports and underwater fishing. The outstanding feature of Sant Francesc Xavier, a town of some 1,000 inhabitants, is its fortified church which, dating from 1726, at one stage was even equipped with artillery so as to afford resistance to pirate attacks. The church interior features a 3-section aisleless nave with apsidal chapels in a right-angled sanctuary. The *fiestas* in honour of the town's patron saint are held on 3rd December. The 8th August sees the commemoration of the conquest of the island, an occasion on which it is traditional, for example, to play a game of bowls (*'tirar a es gall'*).

There are art galleries in Sant Francesc, Es Pujols and along the road to La Savina, whereas shops dealing in handicrafts and jewels are to be found in the capital and at La Mola and El Pilar.

In recent years tourist developments have sprung up around the island's beaches of fine sand and transparent waters, lending Formentera a completely new aspect. Thus, at Es Pujols and San Ferran we find a succession of hotels, apartments, detached houses and bungalows, along with places for entertainment such as pubs and discotheques. The La Mola hotel is situated at Playa de Mitjorn, one of the most popular beaches on the island, alongside that of Es Caló. There are also areas set aside for nudism, although truth be said this activity has never been totally prohibited here, perhaps due to the characteristic non-conformist nature of *Las Pitiusas*.

Illetas beach.

Mitjorn beach.

Cala Sahona.